In Every Season
Memories of Martha's Vineyard

Phyllis Méras

Illustrated by
Thomas H. Cocroft and Robert E. Schwartz

Schiffer Publishing Ltd

4880 Lower Valley Road, Atglen, Pennsylvania 19310
Printed in China

Dedication

For Frances, and in memory of Tom

Cover design: Bruce Waters
Type set in Adobe Jensen/Goudy Oldstyle

ISBN: 978-0-7643-4095-6
Printed in China

Text by Phyllis Méras
Illustrations by Thomas H. Cocroft and Robert E. Schwartz
Much of this material is used courtesy of the *Vineyard Gazette*, where it has appeared in somewhat different forms.

Schiffer Books are available at special discounts for bulk purchases for sales promotions or premiums. Special editions, including personalized covers, corporate imprints, and excerpts can be created in large quantities for special needs. For more information contact the publisher:

Published by Schiffer Publishing Ltd.
4880 Lower Valley Road
Atglen, PA 19310
Phone: (610) 593-1777; Fax: (610) 593-2002
E-mail: Info@schifferbooks.com

For the largest selection of fine reference books on this and related subjects, please visit our website at
www.schifferbooks.com
We are always looking for people to write books on new and related subjects. If you have an idea for a book, please contact us at:
proposals@schifferbooks.com

This book may be purchased from the publisher.
Include $5.00 for shipping.
Please try your bookstore first.
You may write for a free catalog.

In Europe, Schiffer books are distributed by
Bushwood Books
6 Marksbury Ave.
Kew Gardens
Surrey TW9 4JF England
Phone: 44 (0) 20 8392 8585; Fax: 44 (0) 20 8392 9876
E-mail: info@bushwoodbooks.co.uk
Website: www.bushwoodbooks.co.uk

Contents

Acknowledgments

I am grateful to many for their aid and encouragement in the preparation of this book: to Frances and Jane Tenenbaum, Mary Jane Pease, Cynthia Meisner, Bridget Cooke, Anna Alley, Andrew Dickerman, Lynn Christoffers, Nis Kildegaard, Nelson Bryant, Thomas R. Goethals, Richard and Mary Jo Reston, Jerome Kohlberg, Allen Whiting, Julia Wells, Cathy Morris, Robert Oppenheim, Lucy Mitchell, Chris Wallace, Clare Low, Sal Laterra, Ann Nelson, and the late Katharine Tweed.

Beginnings

My Vineyard Homes

In the 1890s, my great-grandfather, a New York City French professor, came to the East Chop Highlands on Martha's Vineyard to teach at the newly founded Martha's Vineyard Summer Institute, one of the first summer schools in the nation. It was begun, its leaders said, "to meet the vacation wants of such who wish to continue the study of some specialty with the rest and recreation of a delightful seaside resort."

He built a red-shingled house with a balcony and a porch all around it. There was a settee that swung back and forth and a big black rocker in a corner. Behind the house, discreetly hidden inside a lattice enclosure, were the big galvanized washtubs and the scrubbing board that were put to use when the family clothes were washed.

The house remains in family hands, but in this modern era, an outdoor shower has replaced the wash yard of the turn of the century. Inside, however, the house is largely unchanged. The coal stove is gone from the kitchen. There is a lavabo upstairs. But in the downstairs bedroom, opposite my grandmother's brass bed, a map of Cottage City, as Oak Bluffs was called when my great-grandfather first came, has hung all these years. The same orange and black dining room chairs sit at the same orange and black dining room table where my great-grandfather sat.

My great-grandfather called the house Mon Repos and by the time I knew him, it was, indeed, his place of summer repose. The Martha's Vineyard Summer Institute, despite having been acclaimed in 1895 as the finest institution of its kind in America, had closed. But Pepé, as we knew him, had decided the Vineyard was to be the family summer home. Now, five generations later, it still is.

Next door to Mon Repos on Arlington Avenue – a monumental name for a very small dirt road – another French professor had a gray-shingled house called Sans Souci. It was there that my father and mother and my brother and I stayed in my earliest Vineyard summers.

Outside were sloping woods that were called the Downs and led to Oak Bluffs. On them, there were nests of fascinating red ants and a hollow where tiger lilies grew. Crossing the Downs on an expedition into town was always a great adventure.

When I was five, we moved to an East Chop house of our own. It had been the Baptist Reception House in the Baptist Camp Meeting Ground in the 1870s. This was a wondrous house, filled with memories for me. On its wide porch, I learned to read. Its attic tower was a perfect place for hiding or haunting. From my bedroom, I could hear the West Chop foghorn bellowing and the bell buoy clanging off East Chop when the wind was right.

In the kitchen, if I had picked blueberries or huckleberries, my grandmother would conjure up scrumptious muffins and cobblers and pies.

Like the Arlington Avenue house, seventy years later, it remains in the family. Clearly, Professor Jean Baptiste Méras, in choosing the Vineyard for his "repose," made the right choice for his descendants, too.

I remember my childhood homes with nostalgia, but there have been Island homes since then that I recall with great fondness, too. The first home my husband, Tom Cocroft (whose drawings help illustrate this book) and I lived in together was the West Tisbury Congregational Church Parsonage. It sits across from the Whiting Farm on the State Road. Though the downstairs bedroom tended to be dank, and the upstairs bedrooms small, there was a hospitable coziness about it.

Outside, rambler roses climbed the fence; a horse chestnut's fragrant blooms plummeted onto the grass in May. Muskrats from the Parsonage Pond came visiting now and then. Raccoons and rabbits frequently nibbled in the garden. Horses grazed in the field below the house, and sometimes, lambs from the Whiting Farm would *baa* mournfully outside our kitchen door. Sadly, after

we had been there eight years, church fathers voted to sell the parsonage.

Shortly after that, we built a house much like the parsonage on the Lagoon in Vineyard Haven. Our house was too far above the Lagoon to hear its waters lapping, but I could see it from the windows, steel gray on stormy mornings, mysteriously swallowed by the fogs of fall, transformed into white ice in winter that heaved and cracked like thunder when the temperature began to rise, and then melted. The perimeter of the Lagoon, which I had known from childhood as a picnicking and swimming place, had shore and woods still wonderful for exploring.

Now I am back in West Tisbury, at the end of a field on Music Street in a house with a bow-shaped roof. I am told that mariners coming home from the sea, but wishing to remember their ships, devised the idea of a roof shaped like an upsidedown ship's hull.

My husband planted apple and cherry and nut trees in our backyard, a blue spruce and lacy locusts and red and yellow roses beside our deck. Since the house sits in a field, and the wind whistles across it in winter, we planted a row of cedar trees before the front door to cut the wind.

In recent years, I have been away from the Vineyard more than I have liked, writing about travel around the world. My husband painted pictures when I was away and tended our two cats. He died in this house some years ago.

This is a book of my decades of memories of Martha's Vineyard before it became the popular summer retreat it is today. It is also a book to acquaint visitors to this 100-square-mile island off Cape Cod to the wonders that it offers. But it is a gentle warning, too, that its natural wonders must be nurtured if coming generations are to enjoy them as five generations of my family have.

Skunk Cabbage Season

Though spring is nearly a month away, there begin to be signs of it. Of course, there are still snow patches on fields and in the woods, but there are also miniature snowdrops in garden beds. In woodland swamps, skunk cabbages, these curious "hermits of the bog," as they are sometimes called, are poking their pointed purple heads up through the snow and melting it around them. They do this by taking oxygen from the soil, even on the coldest of days, and using it to break down sugars and warm themselves. It can, indeed, be thirty degrees F. outside and nearly sixty inside the skunk cabbage. It won't be long now before they will be erupting fully in our swamps and bogs. Although they send forth an unpleasant odor when they are damaged, they are surely a harbinger of the inviting days to come.

And the sun is rising earlier and setting later than it was a month ago. There is less wind when walking an Island beach. Bird songs are more melodious. The courting sounds of mourning doves can be heard and chickadees and nuthatches are beginning to look for nesting places.

Seasonal Vineyard residents have started to e-mail or telephone to their caretakers, asking them to see that all's in order for an Easter visit – that any mice or squirrels that wintered over have been banished to the out-of-doors. Landscapers and house painters and roofers are preparing to go back to work.

Of course, it may still snow, but if it does, the chances are that – like the snow around the skunk cabbage – it will soon melt away. Warm weather, at last, is in sight.

Spring Signs

Now that spring is finally here, I am inclined to get up as soon as the sun bursts through my bedroom windows. Each day there is some new shoot coming up through the cocoa-brown winter carpet of leaves and tawny pine needles.

Skunks have been waddling out of their cold-weather hideaways for some time now. More than a dozen, I understand, have turned up as "unordered" spring stock at Alley's General Store in West Tisbury.

My two cats that spend winters snoozing the days and nights away are alert now at daybreak and eager to be out, their noses a-quiver, their heads cocked, as they hear spring bird songs.

Now that Caitlin Jones and Allen Healy have a huddle of sheep – some black, some white – just over the Chilmark line on the Middle Road, I often walk down there from where I am living now on Music Street in West Tisbury to see how they are doing and to wish them good morning. They are certain to look up inquisitively as I pass and to *baa* what I hope is a welcome (though most likely it is a request for breakfast). In any case, it seems rude not to respond by saying *hello*.

Sometimes, I get to the Healy farm by heading into the woods near Glimmerglass Pond. I am afraid I am not so welcome a passerby to the ducks that are often feeding there as I am to the sheep. Startled, the ducks are likely to scoot away across the brown-gold water.

I have been impatient for spring this year and it has seemed slow in arriving. But when I murmured that disconsolately to my neighbor, Susan Jones, she commented that, for her, this early part of spring is the perfect time – the quiet time she can enjoy before the business of planting begins. And she added that since I was looking for spring signs, I might like to know that she had seen her first piping plover of the season on the beach by Mink Meadows on West Chop.

On Tuesday's walk, I found myrtle sprinkled along the roadsides and daffodil heads turning yellow. Wednesday, Chris Murphy passed me as I walked on the Middle Road, and I asked him what spring signs he had seen. For two weeks, he had been hearing pinkletinks, he said, and the ospreys are back and night crawlers are slithering.

Allen Whiting has lambs and Anne Hopkins two frisky kid goats. Some weeks ago, Johnny Athearn told me to keep my ear a-tuned for the song of the red-winged blackbirds. Lisa Shanor, who tends my garden, has planted peas now, and my flower beds are royal purple with crocuses.

It won't be long now before the summer dwellers arrive and claim woodland paths and riding trails as their own and put up "No Trespassing" signs. But in these first days of spring, they are still at their winter homes and the Vineyard is still all mine!

Redwing

After a Rain

Yesterday morning, I went out from our Lagoon house after the rain. There was a pillow of storm clouds in the sky and the Lagoon, reflecting them, was steely gray. Dave Frantz's black Nashawena, under the lowering sky, looked for all the world like a pirate ship slipped into a hideaway... But, of course, there were no small boats putting out from her, heaped with pieces of eight. On the shore, though, and up in the woods, all sorts of floral spring treasures were to be found, fresh-washed and glistening with raindrops. I discovered a cache of lady's-slippers in a new place – ten of them nodding above their striated leaves. I am not a great admirer of lady's-slippers themselves – I much prefer the name of the flower – but I do like the cool grace of their leaves, and finding new clusters is always a bit like uncovering treasure. They are, after all, orchids, and protected, and in short supply.

Near them, a cluster of sprightly daisies pleased me more, for I like the way a daisy has of capturing sun and holding it in its heart. Even on lowering days, the gold gleams so appealingly from the heart of a daisy. And when one picks daisies and carries them home, they bring sunshine indoors.

Midway on my walk, I met our calico cat out exploring, too, seeking field mice, I suppose, though there is a rabbit about her size who frequents our garden and may, indeed, have a nest somewhere nearby. But it was easy to persuade the calico to come inside for breakfast. Gracefully, she side-stepped all the puddles in the road, stopping just once to wave a paw at a bug diving toward one of the puddles. (The rain had created such deep pools, I almost expected to find a frog splashing about in one… but – like the rowboats I would like to have seen setting out from the Nashawena laden with jewels and gold – splashing frogs were only in my imagination.) The buttercups and the daisies on the roadsides, however, were real, and the plumes of beach grass touched with lavender, and the wild irises.

On Tuesday, I picked a wild iris and was sorry I had, for they close so quickly once picked, and, like the lady's-slipper, they are in short supply.

There were rich pine-needle smells in the woods, and the music of raindrops every now and then as the leaves shook in the wind to dry themselves off. I discovered a copper beech that I had never seen before, and a young birch that the snows of winter had apparently burdened so heavily that it had broken. But I was pleased to see fresh green shoots coming from the base of the trunk, for birches, like wild irises and lady's-slippers, are among the rarer treasures in our Vineyard woods.

After the rain, the mosses seemed especially green – one patch that mingled chartreuse new growth with old brown growth looked almost like the ruffled feathers of a peacock, its blend of colors was so vibrant.

It had been a morning rich in treasures – the absence of the buried kind notwithstanding.

Hooray for the Ice Cream Cone

At last, the ice cream cone has returned to the Vineyard after a long, empty winter!

From Labor Day (or thereabouts) to May, ice cream cones are simply not to be found Up-Island or Down. Occasionally, one surfaces in a convenience store ice cream freezer, but those are hardly the same. Popsicles and chocolate-covered ice cream bars are quite acceptable from a convenience store freezer, but never an ice cream cone. An ice cream cone must be freshly scooped.

Grocery stores, of course, carry ice cream and packaged cones, and with a scoop, one can make one's own ice cream cone at home and eat it there. But that's totally different from getting sticky fingers lapping a cone on Circuit Avenue or while standing in line at the Steamship Authority dock in Vineyard Haven or as one watches the Chappy ferry come and go. And then there are after-the-movie ice cream cones that are the perfect finale to an evening out.

But off-season ice cream cones, as can best be determined, are simply not to be had on the Vineyard.

Surely there are enough winter ice cream-cone lovers on the Island (especially at the prices charged these days for cones) to support at least one ice cream parlor year-round! When Howard Johnson's orange towers covered the country, ice cream cones were available the year-round. In Moscow, even in Communist days – spring, summer, winter – there was street ice cream to be had – carefully weighed out on a scale to make sure that each serving was the same size as the next. And ice cream devotees in fur hats, stamping their feet in the snow, would patiently stand in line for as much as half an hour to savor a scoop of rich, creamy vanilla (the only flavor then available).

Ice cream cone lovers know no seasons. They long only for refreshing ice cream presented in a crunchy cone, to remind them of carefree, happy childhoods.

The Petals of Spring

This is the season of petals. Everywhere that I walk, I am finding carpets of petals beneath my feet. The recent days of rain, of course, have helped lay down these petal carpets. They spread over lawns and fields and roads – snowy white apple blossom, pear blossom, and pink cherry carpets. I am reminded by them of the tale of the Moorish ruler of southern Portugal's Algarve. He married a Scandinavian princess who soon was homesick for snow, it is said, so he planted almond trees so their snow-like, tumbling petals would remind her of home. My apple and pear petal carpets could as easily be seen by an aficionado of winter as a delicate snowfall.

It was, of course, splendid, too, before the petals fell – when West Tisbury apple trees were bowed down with white blooms to be gathered and put in bouquets; when pear blossoms brightened the North Road and cheery pink cherry and peach flowers adorned front yards. But this year, for some reason, I have become particularly conscious of the petals once they have fallen.

Perhaps it is because a month ago, I was at the Ngorongoro Crater Lodge above the Ngorongoro Crater in Tanzania, and one night I opened my lodge door to find that the floor inside had been spread with rose petals and the water that filled the bathtub had been perfumed with rose oil. In a most sybaritic way, in my rose petal-carpeted room, in my bath sprinkled with rose oil, I watched the red African sun sink below the horizon.

Now, of course, on the Vineyard, it is lilac perfume that is sweetening the air and lilac blossoms that are adorning the bushes. Before long, the fragrance of those multiflora roses planted up-Island long ago to be hedges will be filling nostrils and reminding me of the rose perfume of Africa.

Horse chestnut candelabra are replacing the apple and cherry carpets that are beneath my feet. Florida dogwoods are in bloom here and there in Vineyard Haven, but the Kousa dogwood allée at the Polly Hill Arboretum in West Tisbury and the Kousa on the corner of Cooke and School Streets in Edgartown are still to come.

Spring, obviously, has had a long awakening this year, and we have tended to be impatient with it. But I am enjoying seeing its slow stirring as I stroll over my floral carpets.

Mill Pond

After years of absence at the West Tisbury Mill Pond, a pair of swans has taken up residence and appears to be surveying the scene for nesting purposes. An osprey has been sighted perched on a branch above the pond and an otter was observed splashing about by the pond's edge. Over the weekend, earnest youngsters with fishing poles tried their luck catching trout in the recently stocked waters. And there have been sightings of wood ducks.

But before long, they may all be out of luck. The two-acre Mill Pond that was designed in the 19th century to provide water power for the manufacture of textiles is silting up. It has been thirty-eight years since the town last cleared out its muck and weeds and roots. Nowadays, though it is a man-made pond, the West Tisbury Conservation Commission must make sure that no rare species of plant or fish will be destroyed if the pond is dredged the way it used to be.

At a town meeting, voters will be asked to request $50,000 in funding through the Community Preservation Act. The money would be used for investigating what method of dredging would be safest and best for the now barely six-inch deep pond, and to pay for the permits required for dredging.

What a pity it would be if those graceful swans were forced to show off their beauty on some other town's pond and if the otter had to wander off to a more comfortable habitat, too, and if there were no longer fish for young fishermen or the hungry osprey.

And then there is the beauty for human passersby that the silvery Mill Pond offers. It has been a scenic centerpiece for more than a century.

Nov. 5th 1975

Haying Season

June is the season for haying and the sweet fragrance of new-mown hay is everywhere. You can smell it at Nip 'n' Tuck Farm in West Tisbury. You can smell it in Chilmark at Rainbow Farm, and in Edgartown at Morning Glory Farm, and the Farm Institute. And those four are hardly alone on the Vineyard as haymaking sites.

The grass being cut to become hay will probably be timothy with a touch of red clover, but it could be alfalfa or orchard or June grass, rye or fescue, or a mix of them all. And whatever it is, the fragrance will be the same – fresh, sweet, beguiling – and signaling the beginning of summer.

Ideally, haying gets under way as soon as June comes, but, of course, you must make hay while the sun shines and the sun was a questionable visitor until last week. Daily weather reports predicted showers and farmers were hesitant to start mowing for fear the hay would get wet before the work was done. But last week, when it seemed the sun would be staying awhile, every Island farmer with hayfields scurried to get them mowed and his hay crop spread on the field to dry for a day or so, then tedded (fluffed) and baled and stored so it could to be fed to his cows and his sheep and his horses for as long as it lasted.

To most outsiders, it all seems quite romantic, even though for the farmer it can be a hot and gritty job, with scratchy hay going down his collar and the windrows of hay awaiting the baler and stacking crews seeming endless.

The day of the hay wain – the hay wagon – like the day of the hay scythe and the hay rake, is long gone, of course, but trucks piled high with hay bales on which to make wishes (an old Welsh superstition), have been slowing down traffic lately on up-Island roads. Being slowed down by a load of sweet-smelling new-mown hay, however, isn't really much of an inconvenience. Among other things, it's pleasant for most of us (if not for the hardworking farmer) to think that a bit of rural Martha's Vineyard still exists. As for those few impatient sorts who seethe at the tractors and hay trucks on our narrow, winding roads, let them be courteous for these few haymaking weeks.

In August, depending on rainfall, there'll be a second cutting, and the hay will be greener and more tender than this one, the experts say, and perhaps there'll be a third cutting in the fall. But none can equal this first cutting of June that is the harbinger of happy summer days.

Welcome, Summer!

So summer has finally arrived! I know it from the calendar, of course, but even if there were no calendars, I would know it from the perfumes in the air, the soft light over early-morning fields; the happy songs of birds.

I was first alerted to its arrival by the fragrance of the honeysuckle in a West Tisbury hedge I bicycle by each morning. The sweetness yesterday had me stopping, plucking a white and yellow flower from its vine and sucking on it as I remember doing in my childhood. I remember honeysuckle then being tastier than yesterday's was, but perhaps yesterday's had been in bloom too long or my adult taste buds are jaded. It really never was the taste of honeysuckle that mattered anyway, it was that all-encompassing fragrance.

There is great promise in the perfume of honeysuckle – promise of carefree summer days, of sunning on Island beaches, stargazing on clear nights, watching the dancing of fireflies, swimming in up-Island ponds shimmering with phosphoresce after dark.

There is promise of breezes for sailing, of bluefish jumping. A goldfinch darted over my bicycle this morning to let me know that the birds of summer should never be forgotten. A neighbor tells me she has seen an all-too-rare quail on a West Tisbury dirt road. The water lilies are in bloom on Glimmerglass Pond.

Now that summer is here, Islanders are readying cottages and camps for rental. The cars arriving on the Steamship Authority ferry are laden with bicycles and kayaks and tennis rackets and energetic young sorts eager to use them.

Summer, for some, is rocking chair, glider, hammock, and swing time. These slow motion activities, I suppose, are inviting because they are not demanding on hot summer days. Like the fragrance of honeysuckle, there is a gentleness to them.

Summer is picnic time in a piney wood, beach party time. For the very young, it is Flying Horses time in Oak Buffs; for older brothers and sisters, it is a time for adventure and exploration, for building rafts and tree houses, for bicycling on leafy up-Island roads in Chilmark and Aquinnah. School is over. There are so many better things to do than sit in stuffy classrooms!

Of course, before we know it, the Fourth of July parade in Edgartown and the Tisbury Street Fair will have come and gone; Illumination Night will have brightened the Methodist Camp Ground in Oak Bluffs; the sights and the sounds of the Agricultural Fair in West Tisbury – the jars of jellies and pickles and jams, the mooing of cattle and neighing of horses – will be over.

It's a pity summer is such a short season, but while it is here, it should be enjoyed to the fullest. I am grateful to the honeysuckle for reminding me not to miss a day of it.

Cocroft
Nov 4, '57

Edgartown Fences

June is the month for sprucing up Edgartown fences – doing touch-ups with paint in preparation for summer. On North and South Water Streets, North and South Summer, Cooke and Cottage, fences are getting a fresh, new look. Often, these are old-fashioned white picket fences with spikes, or they may be without the spikes and "capped" with a board along the top. The latter, it is said, are known as Edgartown fences. Some say those are just right for the town's tall, grand captains' houses, while the fences with pickets add stature to the smaller cottages.

Edgartown fences lend themselves particularly admirably to showing off climbing roses, for the roses can grow horizontally along the bar and then tumble over the top.

But all sorts of flowers are shown to advantage behind a freshly painted white fence – plump blue hydrangeas are nicely set off by a picket fence as are peonies and day lilies. Pink and purple clematis, like the climbing roses, cascades colorfully on the flat-topped Edgartown fence.

But there are also lattice fences in Edgartown. They usually top board fences that enclose grand private gardens. The lattice allows the curious passerby to peak through and get just a glimpse of the floral wonders behind. And here and there, there are rail fences, too, but less rustic ones than those to be found in West Tisbury and Chilmark. They are fashioned of whole logs rather than split rails.

Now and then, one sees a low stone wall or a brick wall separating garden from street, and even – in front of the Charlotte Inn on South Summer Street – a wrought-iron fence painted dark shutter green to keep it inconspicuous among plantings.

But it's the white fences of Edgartown that are so proudly showing off now.

Crow Antics

Anyone who is out early in the morning these early summer days will surely hear or see a crow, or a murder of crows, as groups of crows are called. They may be cawing from one tree to the next, alerting each other to the skunk dead in the road below or the field new-planted with tasty seed corn. They may simply be conversing. But there is always an urgency in the voice of a crow.

Naturalists say that, along with parrots, members of the crow family (these include blue jays, magpies, and ravens), are the most intelligent of the birds. Crows are not averse to being tamed either – perhaps they know instinctively that if they are man's friend, he will be their friend, too. A handful of shiny coins laid down on a path or road where they glitter in the sun is a good way of attracting a crow.

Some years ago, though in different decades, two tame crows lived in West Tisbury and if their owners were out, they would boldly make the rounds of neighboring houses where they would be fed in exchange for performing crow-like antics.

Farmers, of course, don't like crows – particularly because of their predilection for seed corn and tomatoes. And crows are picky about the tomatoes they eat, always sampling before they decide which tomato is the tastiest. A crow-pecked tomato is hardly one a farmer can sell.

Time was when scarecrows of varying charm were put out in Vineyard fields to keep crows away. The late Albert and Peg Littlefield had a scarecrow family in West Tisbury. Dapper Dan in a morning coat, striped trousers, a cravat and a top hat; his wife, Lucy and their yellow-yarn-haired daughter warned crows away from their State road garden by waving pie pans in the wind.

But now scarecrows seem largely a thing of the past. Occasionally, Morning Glory farm in Edgartown sets one up and Tom Hodgson in West Tisbury has a truly scary one on Tiasquam Road that wears crow and turkey feathers in his hat and a Halloween mask in place of a face.

But more often today, netting over the tomato plants and glittering metallic tape have replaced the scarecrows of yore. At the Norton Farm in Vineyard Haven, those are the anti-crow tactics. But even farmers like the Nortons are grudgingly impressed with the intelligence of crows. Did you know, Sonya Norton asks, that a sentinel crow can differentiate between a farmer walking, a farmer with a stick, and a farmer with a gun, and caw his warning to his comrades accordingly?

Jan 14th 1970

Benches

In summer, Island benches are filled with sitters. There are benches on overlooks and benches in parks, benches in woods and benches in towns, and, of course, there are benches at Vineyard Transit Authority stops.

Some benches are set on wrought-iron legs and may even have elaborate wrought-iron backs. Some have seats constructed of slats. Some – usually memorial benches – are of stone and may be backless. Among Island memorial benches is one to Henry Beetle Hough at Sheriff's Meadow in Edgartown. It looks out over Sheriff's Meadow Pond, John Butler's Mud Hole, and Nantucket Sound. At this time of year, a keen-eyed occupant of that bench may see a painted turtle climbing up from the mud hole and burying eggs in the grass. There also are Edgartown memorial benches to tennis player and Harborside Boatyard manager David Chase near the town tennis courts.

In West Tisbury, a memorial bench to longtime-selectman Allen M. Look has a view of the still waters of the Mill Pond. Then at Cedar Tree Neck, there are memorial benches. There is another to Sheriff's Meadow founder Henry Beetle Hough, and one to Oak Bluffs summer dweller Peter C. Gardner that affords an unobstructed view across Vineyard Sound. An Ames family bench overlooks Ames Pond. There are undoubtedly others across the Island that are tributes to individuals that have been missed.

Along Edgartown's Main Street, wooden benches are put to good use in winter as well as summer. Frequenters tend to be locals interested in the comings and goings of their neighbors and in catching up with local gossip.

On South Summer and North Water Streets are benches for enjoying ice cream and sandwiches or for sipping coffee or a cold drink. Before library reconstruction began, there was a bench dedicated to Maurita Prada where the impatient could start reading the volume they had just checked out.

In Edgartown, there are also benches across from the Harbor View. From these, early birds can watch the sun rise over Cape Pogue and the Edgartown Light. The comings and goings of boats in the harbor can be followed from wharf benches.

Oak Bluffs has a sizable complement of benches. There are those for yacht-watchers along Lake Anthony, while just across from Ocean Park, a bench affords a view of the ferry arriving and departing. And, of course, there are benches just for enjoying the park's floral plantings or taking an afternoon snooze. Such benches are a good place to tie shoelaces.

East Chop has a bench behind the lighthouse for those who like to watch the sailboats in the Sound. And West Chop has one at the flagpole for seeing the sun set over the Middle Ground. From the Owen Park benches in Vineyard Haven, there is splendid moon-viewing.

On windy days, bench-sitters at Aquinnah Park can see the combers of the Atlantic in the distance and seagulls swooping.

In Menemsha, the dockside benches are perfectly situated to keep an eye on fishing boats and sail and motor yachts. They are also fine for cracking open fresh-boiled lobsters from the Mememsha Fish Market or Larsen's and picnicking.

Outside Leslie's Drugstore in Vineyard Haven and in front of the Bunch of Grapes Bookstore bench sitters can watch the police slip tickets under the windshield wipers of scofflaws who overstay parking limits.

Sometimes, a bench may cease to be appreciated if sat on too long. (Martha's Vineyard Regional High School graduation attendees should remember to take a plump cushion as well as a camera to the annual festivities at the Tabernacle in Oak Bluffs.) But one generally doesn't look to benches for long-term comfort anyway. They are for short-term use and enjoyment.

And what we would miss if we had to do without them!

In Praise of Beach Days

To the beach, to the beach these hot summer days! It doesn't matter what beach or what time of day. What matters is taking advantage of cool water and stretches of sand that are clean and inviting.

There are those fortunate few whose homes are on the water and who can plunge into it as soon as they are out of bed on a summer morning. Menemsha and Chilmark Ponds, the Lagoon, Lake Tashmoo, Squibnocket, Uncle Seth's Pond and Edgartown's Fuller Street Beach all lend themselves to such early morning plunges. The water is especially invigorating then and there is no better way to start a summer day. Depending upon the choice of beach, one may see cormorants drying their wings on a raft, earnest ducks fishing for breakfast, terns angered at human intrusion, or a sluggish horseshoe crab.

But early morning is not the only time to enjoy Island sand and water. Toward mid-day, if one likes company, there will be plenty of it at the Bend-in-the Road Beach between Oak Bluffs and Edgartown, or at Katama or below the dunes along Moshup's Trail in Aquinnah. Children at the Bend-in-the-Road will jump up and down in glee at the water's edge. And, running into it, swim and spout like whales until they are blue with cold. Handsome youths, who generally prefer surf to the lapping waters of the Sound, will be diving through the breakers at Edgartown's South Beach with grace and agility, or surf-boarding.

And then there is the afternoon beach contingent. After marketing and other chores have been attended to, these swimmer-sunners will head for the water to cool off. Perhaps they will snooze a little on the sand, or work up an appetite for dinner by swimming a lap or two to a destination like a jetty or a moored boat.

Evening swimming should certainly not be forgotten, either. In the evening, when moonlight streams over Chilmark's Quitsa Pond or the Lagoon and phosphorescence dances, those two ponds are at their most enticing. There is that same stillness of early morning.

And so the cry of summer is: "Off to the beach!"

After the Fourth of July

The Fourth of July has come and gone and full-fledged summer is here. One knows it, of course, because of the cars and the people. But one knows it in subtler ways, too. Shell pink and magenta Rosa rugosa blooms are studding dunes and hillsides. The sojourn of the perky daisies of June is gradually coming to a close, their early summer visit ended.

Orange day lilies and tiger lilies and yellow coreopsis are in the fields now and by the roadsides. I have just seen my first blue chicory of the season. The other morning I picked a cluster of the pungent yarrow that, I am told, was used by Achilles to treat the wounds of his soldiers.

I discover such odd facts annually when summer comes and I have idle moments. Then I tend to pull books of garden folklore out of a bookcase and browse in them. Two other curious garden notes of summer that I have just gleaned from my peripatetic reading concern roses and peaches.

Although my roses did surprisingly well in June, the leaves are yellowing now. I have learned that if I put banana peels in the ground under them, the peels will supply magnesium, calcium, sulfur, potassium, sodium, and silica to the roses. The lack of any one of these may be the cause of my rose problem. As for the peaches, I have discovered that if a peach appears on my peach tree this summer (last summer, I had a single peach), festooning the tree with mothballs will prevent leaf curl.

This past spring, I was riding my vintage bicycle mornings, rather than walking. I was readying for a trip to Jordan. There I knew there was to be rock-climbing aplenty involved in the sightseeing, and endless walking in Middle East heat, so I bicycled six miles a day in preparation.

Though my rusty, creaky old bike travels slowly, thereby allowing me to absorb Vineyard landscape from it in a way that I never could on a 10-speeder, nonetheless, walking is better for Vineyard-viewing of flora and fauna. The rabbit that lives in my front field, for example, is terrorized by the sound of my creaking bicycle and frantically rushes from side to side of the road to try to escape it.

And had I been cycling yesterday, I could never have found the first ripe blueberries of this July, nestled in their dark leaves on an embankment. Though it was hardly a great cache of them that I found, I picked enough to sprinkle on my breakfast cereal. Nor would I have noticed the holly tree on the Middle Road that surely has been there for years, but I have been missing it. I often miss the sounds of summer – the whispering of leaves, the soughing of pines, the whistling, the calling, the cooing of the birds as I creak down a road on my bicycle.

Yesterday morning, on foot, I could walk into the woods, too, for a closer look at the dappled leaves and the moss patterns on the rocks. I have yet to get my little Edgartown beach boat – or even my rowboat – into the water for full enjoyment of the season. I have taken only one swim. But this is only the first week of July, after all. Nearly two full months of summer still lie ahead.

Blueberries

Missing Birds

For more than 50 years, ducks have bobbed and swans gracefully slipped across the waters of West Tisbury's Mill Pond. But since this past spring, both the ducks – mallards and mottled Muscovies – and gray and white barnyard geese that had called the Mill Pond home recently, have been missing.

The swans reigned supreme, gliding their way up and down the pond, nesting along its banks and proudly preening for visitors enjoying the view from the Allen M. Look memorial bench that honors that late West Tisbury selectman.

Cars crossing the bridge would slow down this summer looking for the geese and ducks, and youngsters who came with bread to the old feeding grounds beside the renovated police station were disappointed to find no feathered creatures waiting hungrily to be fed.

But those who have been worrying about the birds' whereabouts (were they all run down by thoughtless motorists or shot in hunting season?) need worry no longer. It turns out the pond's denizens have been doing swimmingly (even if elsewhere) former Police Chief George Manter reports.

Most of the Muscovites now make their home with other Muscovites in Police Officer Skip Manter's barnyard on the Manter Farm down New Lane.

As for the geese, Animal Control Officer Joan Jenkinson says proudly that a gray Mill Pond goose and gander, now owned by Liz Thompson of Northern Pines, were Blue Ribbon winners at the Agricultural Fair, while some of the whites have found a happy home with Harold and Marjorie Rogers at Indian Hill and others with the Dunkl family of Chilmark. All have multiplied. And now that fall is in the air, Joan Jenkinson adds, it is likely that some of the transient mallards will be coming back. Meanwhile, she rather likes having the pond as a rehab center for birds that come her way in time of need. Right now these include a swan with an injured wing and an elderly Canada goose to which she is giving Tender Loving Care.

Charitable that surely is, but it isn't the same as the longtime feeders at the Mill Pond feel, as having a flock of quacking ducks and a gaggle of hissing geese waiting to greet them every day on the police station green. For them, the absence of their feathered friends – even if they weren't always the cleanest of creatures – means one more piece of the old Vineyard is gone.

June 1st 1967

Apr. 1977

Summer Refreshments

Summer is the season for lemonade and iced tea days – hot, muggy days when nothing is quite so thirst-quenching as a tall, cool glass of one of those beverages. Of course, they're old-fashioned drinks. The ice cream soda is a more modern concoction that serves the same purpose – but not quite. Ice cream sodas are filling and lemonade and iced tea are not.

Both can be quickly and efficiently made nowadays with powder from a jar. The sweetener (frequently artificial, and therefore virtually non-caloric) is already in, along with – in both cases – the lemon flavor. And in a pinch, the bottled powder will do, mixed with cold water and ice on a sticky day.

However, a genuine lemonade with fresh-squeezed lemon and some rind in it really is much better – though to be properly done, the sugar and water that are mixed with the lemon juice really should be boiled together first. And that's time-consuming, and hot, on a day that is already hot.

But lemonade mixed in a frosted glass pitcher and sipped through decorative glass straws under a shade tree on a lawn – what could be better? Iced tea, maybe, brewed extra-strong from a good black Indian tea to allow for dilution when ice is added, and served in the same sort of tall glasses as the lemonade, with a slice of lemon and a sprig of fresh mint with a plate of fresh ginger cookies on the side.

It's interesting to note that iced tea, though an Englishman's invention, had its debut in America at the 1904 St. Louis World's Fair. It was hot as blazes that year in St. Louis and no one was drinking the hot tea at the concessions. But when the imaginative concessionaire added ice, the crowds came flocking. Of course. There's caffeine in tea, which makes drinking it exhilarating even on dog days.

Either way – the lemonade or the iced tea way – you can't go wrong in summer.

Music Street Trees

Last Monday evening, the West Tisbury Planning Board held a hearing at Howes House to weigh the fate of four venerable town oak trees. One has stood for a century diagonally across the road from the Robert Morgenthaus' house at the entrance to the Middle Road. Another, a decade or so younger, stands tall across the way. Up the Panhandle, two others stretch their limbs over the road, shading it for cyclists and walkers on hot summer days – serving as a runway for squirrels in all seasons, a resting place for crows, a tapping site for woodpeckers.

Most mornings and some evenings, summer and winter, I walk up Music Street to the Panhandle. In summer, the canopy overhead shields me from both sun and rain, although if a breeze shakes the trees on rainy or misty days, I am likely to find myself slightly dampened by a refreshing shower.

In fall, I watch those summer leaves turn bronze and tumble down. On fine days, just after the sun comes up, and before cars scatter the riches, Music Street and the Panhandle seem to be royal roads, all paved in bronze. A little later in the season, the oak leaves are a warm chestnut brown mingling with the russet of maples and the lemon yellow of birches.

Then winter comes, and the tree limbs are elephant gray with a faint tinge of pink on snowy days.

The grandest trees of Music Street, of course, are at the McCulloughs' and the Wassermans' and Sophie Block's, but the ones whose fate lay with the Planning Board are grand trees, too, even if they are younger and less imposing. It is the trees, the bends, the scraggly pavement here and there, the stone walls edging woods and fields that make West Tisbury roads – the North Road, the Middle Road, Music Street, the Panhandle – so very special.

The Agricultural Fair, the Farmers' Market, and the Artisans' Fair are gala events of summer, but the white steeple of the Congregational Church, the porch at Alley's, the captains' houses along Music Street – and the trees that bow and sigh and whisper are with West Tisbury folk year-round. Now, in the interest of big trucks, big buses, and road safety, we were being told, four trees that have edged the road for generations needed to be felled. Happily, petitioners against their going weighed in with sufficient strength – and for another year, at least the trees are safe.

Island Ponds

I have been exploring Island ponds lately – Squibnocket and the Lagoon in the early morning; Like Tashmoo at twilight, and comparing flora and fauna and vistas. Squibnocket, being most remote, is richest in wildlife. A friendly otter, the other day, splashed happily about when friends and I went canoeing. He seemed eager for recognition and a breakfast crumb or two, if one were to be had. But when it wasn't, he simply ducked his whiskers underwater again in search of something fishy and tasty in the depths of the pond, and was gone.

And there were sedate swans sailing in fleets and Canada geese feeding and snowy egrets and young osprey could be seen through the binoculars high on nesting poles. For some years now, Gus Ben David and his Felix Neck Wildlife Sanctuary associates have been erecting nesting poles across the Island to lure the osprey back. They have been fast disappearing as development intrudes on their marshy nesting places.

We looked for snapping turtles, for they are said to be Squibnocket denizens, too, but there were none to be seen. The flora, however, was abundant. There was viburnum, loosestrife, white clusters of yarrow, and sunbursts of evening primroses. The houses that we passed tended to be grand, sprawling structures on the hills and shore. At Lake Tashmoo at sundown, an egret waded; horseshoe crabs had shed their crisp brown shells and left them on the sand, and a child had forgotten small blue sneakers there beside them.

Mid-pond on the flats, quahaugers dug and called back and forth to each other about their progress, Sailboats and powerboats bobbed cozily at their moorings after a day's busy activity.

cocroft - 47

There seemed more marshy lands at Tashmoo than around the Lagoon with which I am more familiar – more marshy places that wet my feet as I circled the shore. As for the dwellings, they were on a smaller scale than Squibnocket's – at least those I viewed in the neighborhood of the town landing.

This morning, I went from Vineyard Haven to Oak Bluffs around the Lagoon. It is a frequent morning stroll of mine. There is a swan family at the Oak Bluffs pumping station pond, and one of the swans had flown across the causeway and – long-necked and proud – was looking imperiously at the seagulls and the cormorants that are the Lagoon's permanent inhabitants. Resplendent, the swan swam by the raft where the cormorants dry their wings after their breakfast diving. The swan is so regal a creature; the cormorant so plain, but they seemed quite undismayed by being sneered at – or so it seemed. The cormorants simply continued to flap their wings and stretch their scrawny necks.

Two mallards swam purposefully out from the sedge at the edge if the pond, leaving strong wakes the way ducks do; I startled a nest of birds in a tall tree and their dismayed twittering was rather like the squeaking of a saw, it seemed to me. I was curious as to what birds they were. We have crows aplenty here in the Lagoon woods and this summer we have yellow flycatchers nesting and cardinals coming and going.

Once, there were mourning doves cooing and sometimes at night a whip-poor-will calls or an owl hoots, but the squeaking saw sound was new to me.

I found two whelk shells on the beach and half an eel and wondered if both were abandoned bait of some young fisherman's, for I have never seen either before at the Lagoon. I noticed the dusty miller had grown tall stalks with tiny pods filled with brown seeds. Since there is only one patch of dusty miller on our shore, I snipped off three pods and broke them open and scattered their contents as I walked.

The watercress is as effulgent as always where fresh water streams spring from the banks and tumble down to the beach.

From under a nest of boats in front of the Culins', a white-tailed rabbit hopped, then froze as I passed by – its ears and nose twitching, eyes darting.

Beyond the Frantzes, a rubber Zodiac was hauled up and with its pointed pontoons looked almost like some strange animal from Mars crouched, ready to spring waterwards.

The homes fronting the Lagoon, like the Tashmoo houses, tend to be more the summer camp sort than in the grand house style of those fronting on Squibnocket. Sometimes they are nestled in the oaks and pines; sometimes they perch on shore. For the first time, I noticed that we have Lagoon-front apple trees growing.

And my pond explorations are just beginning. There are Sengekontacket, Quitsa, Oyster Pond, the Great Ponds, James's Pond, Glimmerglass, and so many other ponds to visit.

View from the Porch

Once upon a time, depending on where you lived, you built porches to sit on in fine weather and watch your neighbors pass by. And you would nod to them, and probably gossip about them, too.

You rocked on a porch, and if you were fortunate enough to have an Island home overlooking the Sound, so much the better – you didn't rely on your neighbors alone to watch. You watched the sun set as you rocked. It was crimson, apricot, pink, depending on the month and the weather. And you watched the

water change in color, too, from silver in the morning sun to lead gray on stormy days or the deep dark green the walls of Davy Jones's locker must surely be, or to turquoise and cobalt blue, and gold in the moonlight.

If you were an Island visitor in those days, you might have sat out on the porch of the Pawnee House on Oak Bluffs' Circuit Avenue and smelled the popcorn and taffy smells from Darling's Old Popcorn Store. And you would have watched the Circuit Avenue strollers.

Nowadays, the Wesley House in Oak Bluffs and the Harbor View in Edgartown continue to have porches with fine, big rockers. The latter has a clear view of the lighthouse below. But, for the most part, porches are a thing of the past. And rocking chairs are, too, except for those people with back problems who rock in them purposefully, not lackadaisically the way a rocker is meant to be rocked.

Canvas-backed director's chairs and chairs with webbed plastic seats have taken the place of rockers as decks have replaced the porches of yore. Decks are more "with it" somehow than porches are – perhaps because they relate to the sport of boating and there are so many yachtsmen about.

Decks may or may not have a railing – porches always did. Decks, like as not, are stained, not painted. Porches were always freshly painted every summer or two. Porches tended to have roofs over them to protect you from the sun. Decks have no roofs, for though physicians question too much exposure to the sun nowadays, most people continue to enjoy basking in it.

And that leads to the most important difference of all between a porch and a deck. A porch (except for the overlooking-the-sea sort) was most often facing onto a public place and passersby were an important part of the enjoyment a porch afforded. Decks tend to be on the backs of houses where one can stretch out and tan and have private cookouts. That's too bad. There was something very sociable about a porch.

Roses in Bloom

All over the Island, roses are in bloom and their fragrance is mellowing the summer air. Proper climbing roses – pink and red, white and yellow – are showing off in Edgartown. Wild roses – Rosa rugosa – with their sunny yellow centers and slightly fuzzy dark green leaves, are nestled in the State Beach grass in Oak Bluffs, at Aquinnah's West Basin, and on West Tisbury and Chilmark embankments. Rosa rugosa is a native of Japan, brought to America by seamen long ago.

The petals of white Multiflora rose clusters are floating to the ground and carpeting our roads. Multiflora roses have their admirers and their detractors. They are loved by some for the way they spread – along a fence, at the foot of a bird feeder, or climbing a barn wall. Sometime in the past, they were introduced to Vineyard farms to edge the fields, but they got out of hand and soon were growing in the fields, not just bordering them. Those who dislike them are the proper gardeners who often clear them away to make room for more sedate plants.

Before long, Rosa rugosa will stop blooming and will be forming orange-red rose hips which, for the industrious willing to cook them and strain out their many seeds, will make a tart jelly rich in vitamin C.

But it is the romance of the rose, of course that makes it so important. The gift of a rose, it is said, is a gift of love. From the smooth, soft petals of the rose, the Bulgarians, in particular, make attar of roses. This, properly combined with other ingredients, becomes the most seductive and expensive of perfumes.

The very first rose to grow, according to a medieval tale, sprouted in Bethlehem when an innocent maiden, accused as a witch by a spurned lover, was sentenced to be burned at the stake. But God intervened. The stake budded and the maiden stood unharmed beneath a canopy of red and white rose blossoms.

All hail the rose!

Remember the Clover

CLOVER

Poor clover. It tends to be forgotten when the showier wildflowers of summer are in bloom – except by the rabbits and raccoons that thrive on it. And by those persevering sorts seeking a four-leaf clover to bring good fortune.

For centuries, of course, the four-leaf clover has been sought for that. Tradition has always had it, for example, that the maiden who puts a four-leaf clover in her shoe will marry the first man whom she meets, while she who eats a four-leaf clover will wed the first man whose hand she shakes. (Realistically – if realism plays any part in all of this – eating the clover seems a wiser move than putting it in one's shoe. At least one has some control over whose hand one shakes.)

But four-leaf clovers are hard to come by, and while they surely can be found in Vineyard meadows, it is the three-leaf variety that most people see – or pass by quickly without seeing.

The three-leaf kind is not without its myths and legends, too. It took its name, it is said, from the fact that its three leaves resembled the Greek clava – the three-knobbed club of the mythical Greek hero, Hercules. And it is that same three-leaf clover that designates the club suit in a deck of playing cards.

And then there are the flowers of the clover to consider. Both white and red clover blossoms, dried, were once used to brew a healthful tea. The red blossoms (lavender-pink is what they really are) reportedly keep the moths away from furs, and with honey and onions added – if one likes – the tea made from them will relieve coughs and hoarseness.

So there's more to clover than meets the eye. And it should not be slighted.

Summer's Green Triumphal Arches

There are few lovelier sights in an Island summer than tree arches across a road. The North Road, the Middle Road in Chilmark, the Oak Bluffs – Edgartown Road beyond Cow Bay – have fine examples of them. Most often it is oaks that gently touch each other's limbs across a road, and cool it and make patterns on it with their shadows. Before Dutch elm disease, it was the elm's limbs that arched in many places.

Architects, of course, have fashioned arches through the ages – rounded Roman and Norman ones, the pointed Gothic, the Moorish that is rounded and pointed both. And there are grand triumphal arches. Berlin has its Brandenburg Gate, the symbol of the city. And Paris has its Arch of Triumph, 150 feet in height, 135 in breadth, 69 in depth, it is the largest of the world's triumphal arches, and is embellished with sculpted allegories recording all the victories of Napoleon I.

There is no need for embellishing tree arches. Their leaves – restless in wind – are sometimes right side up and deepest green, and sometimes, in the rain, turned upsidedown, they are a softer hue. Against the sky, leaf outlines are like the most delicate of laces.

Of course, the limbs of arches snap against the roofs of tourist buses, and sometimes drivers and passengers alike complain. But whenever they feel inclined to make a complaint, they should step out and walk – not ride – along a woodsy Island road; look up, admire, and recognizing beauty, feel triumphant.

My Yellow Cat and I

We have been best friends for thirteen years, my Yellow Cat and I. We have explored the Lagoon woods in Vineyard Haven together, walked its beach – her tiny paw prints in the sand beside my oafish sneaker prints.

We have chased butterflies in West Tisbury fields and played hide and seek in the tall grasses. Now, for two weeks, she has been missing, and I have been walking alone in the grass – imagining when I see Queen Anne's lace that it is the plume of her tail and finding her golden head in every plume of goldenrod.

We met at Gloria Norton's in Edgartown when the Yellow Cat was only six weeks old – hardly a cat then, but she has always been called the Yellow Cat to differentiate her from her cousin, Groucho, the calico cat, who also lived with us.

Her proper name in veterinary records is Little Red, but she has never been red and it is years since she has been little. When she left Edgartown to move with us to the West Tisbury parsonage and seemed peckish about eating, Phyllis Smith at Alley's General Store, suggested that she might like baby food. So Little Red began to grow, and grew mightily, on a diet that consisted largely of chicken and turkey, and lamb and beef baby food.

She spent a happy kittenhood in the vegetable garden at the parsonage where we lived. She hid among the cornstalks, batted at the pink and blue sweet peas with a golden paw, wiggled expectantly in anticipation of pouncing on mice. But she rarely, if ever, caught one. I hope now that she is on her own, that she is doing better than that.

Hunting has never been a particular pastime of hers. Squirrels and rabbits may have looked inviting to her, but she never managed to tackle any of them. She watched them, tirelessly.

Clearly, they felt secure despite the Yellow Cat's riveting stare and trembling haunches. Never in her life has she managed to catch a bird.

She liked living on the Lagoon where she had the beach to stroll on and neighbors to visit. She was never quite forgiven at our house for walking down the dirt road to Marian Halperin's one Thanksgiving afternoon when we had shooed her away from the Thanksgiving table until the guests had been served. She meowed piteously at Marian's door and, of course, she was invited in for turkey and giblets and ate so ravenously that it seemed as if she was never fed at home. In reality, in addition to baby food, the Yellow Cat was living sumptuously on assorted cat foods, chicken livers, fish, and half and half.

The favorite toy of her early years (in addition to crackly Camels cigarette wrappers) was a George Magnuson duck decoy. Grabbing its bill between her forepaws, she would wrestle endlessly with it on the kitchen floor. Tail-chasing on the high deck railing above the Lagoon was another favorite game of hers, guaranteed to terrify those watching her twirl precariously twenty feet above the ground.

The Yellow Cat had been chosen to be a companion for her calico relative – also a Norton cat offspring, though a year older, but Groucho had never really wanted a companion. It was simply that humans thought she ought to have one. The Yellow Cat tried desperately to become friends with Groucho, chasing her, playing with her tail when the older cat was eating, but she was always spurned with a low growl. The pair never fought. The calico was simply disdainful of her less elegant, more obstreperous, and (she seemed to think) none-too-bright golden cousin.

It was true that the Yellow Cat, for all the fluffiness of her fur and its glowing golden color, lacked the regal look of the tri-colored, silky (if not fluffy) calico, but she was handsome all the same.

Quasi-nameless as the Yellow Cat has been, friends have always tried naming her. One friend, regarding her broad posterior as she crouched over a meal one day, dubbed her, insultingly, the Meatloaf. Another visitor called her Big Bushy after her full white-tipped tail. A third thought she resembled shortbread in color and nicknamed her that. But no name but the Yellow Cat or the Little Cat (harking back to the short period of time when she was littler than Groucho) ever took. She never answered to a name anyway. Doglike, she has always responded to a whistle, followed, if I was the one calling her, by all sorts of terms of endearment – Muffin, Pumpkin, Puss, Dear Cat, Kitten Cat.

She spent one winter beyond Norton Circle at the Rogers' House at the end of the Indian Hill Road in West Tisbury. There, the stone walls proved endlessly fascinating to her. They were splendid for sunning, excellent for bird-watching, not bad at all for mouse-watching. She liked the pinkletinks in the swamp, there, not to eat, but – like all of us – to listen to. She was clearly delighted by occasional visits of plump young quail. And the rabbits and squirrels there, of course, like their Lagoon cousins, were an endless distraction.

The Yellow Cat has lived in the Bow House at the back of a field on Music Street in West Tisbury for a year and two months now, quite happily, as far as she has let anyone know. This past Thanksgiving, she was put to the test by the arrival of two tiger kittens that came to her house to stay. In the same way that her calico relative was not pleased with her arrival, no more has she been pleased to have such ordinary newcomers sharing what she had hoped would be exclusively her bed and board. (The calico died two years ago.)

She has spat at the kittens accordingly, and whacked at them occasionally in a fit of pique as they – as she used to do with the calico – tickled her extended tail at dinnertime. But they all seemed to have made their peace, and while she would have preferred it had they never arrived, they have been tolerated.

And she and I have continued our rambles and walks – on which I have responded with talking to her somewhat asthmatic purr. But this summer, I have been away for six weeks. She has been well tended and fed, all the same. Though my husband has always shared Groucho's disdain for the Yellow Cat, he has patted her occasionally, fed her when she looked hungry, let her sit near him when he worked in the garden, opened and closed doors behind her.

But last week when I came home from a journey that was two weeks longer than my usual travels, I learned that the Yellow Cat was gone. In the hot days of these recent weeks, she had spent more and more time outdoors, my husband said. Then, one day, she had not come home at all, nor the next day, nor the day after.

So I have been walking the fields and woods that she and I walked together by myself these days, whistling and calling, calling and whistling, murmuring promises that if she will come home, I will not leave her for so long a time again.

I have been scanning the clover and the brown-eyed Susans, following the route of the Tiasquam River, calling her, knocking on strangers' doors and looking into strangers' barns for her. I have been posting notices on trees and fences and advertising in the newspapers for my golden friend. All sorts of people have been kind and hoped they had found her for me – the lifeguard at Seth's Pond, a Chilmark summer visitor who brought me a golden cat in her car, so certain she was it was the Yellow Cat, West Tisbury's Animal Control Officer, the West Tisbury police.

And I still think the Yellow Cat is out there somewhere catching grasshoppers and maybe an occasional mouse in the grass, and wishing I would come home so she could prance beside me again and purr asthmatically in my ear.

I have done the best I can to let her know I am home, waiting so we can play together.

The Seasons of Spiders

Spring and summer and fall are spider seasons in garages and cellars, on porches and decks, in the garden. Indoors, brooms are kept busy sweeping webs from here and there. But in the garden, no sweeping needs to be done, and on damp mornings, our woods and fields are aglitter with dewdrop-bedecked webs for the walker to pause and admire. And surely there is much to admire in the delicacy and intricacy of a spider's web. Scotland's Robert the Bruce is said to have taken heart and returned to battle the English after watching the persistence with which a spider was weaving its web. But its artistry, as well as its creative persistence, is worth our praise.

Each species builds after its own design. Some webs are simply a tangle; some funnel-shaped; some like hammocks; some look like writing; the garden spider creates cartwheels of silken circles with spokes.

For all the delicacy of design and transparency of the spider's web, they are extraordinarily strong, as is apparent when the wind blows and the threads of a web simply billow a little, but hold fast. Now and then, spider's thread being as strong as it is, man has sought to make use of it in garments. In eighteenth-century France, it is said, one inventive gentleman managed to fashion stockings and mittens from spider's silk, another to collect some on a spool. But the thread is so fine it defies any commercial weaving. So spider's silk-silvery and gleaming must simply be admired in the morning garden. That's all right, too.

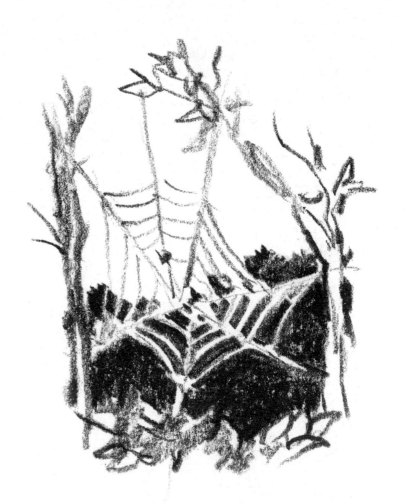

Blackberry Blossoms

It will be almost autumn before the blackberries are ripe, but the woods are full of their blossoms these days – pretty little white flowers not unlike wild roses in miniature. They are rambling along stone walls, and climbing banks, and inviting passersby to stop to pick them – until the passersby stop and are stopped in turn by the brambles that guard the blackberries.

When the flowers are gone, and the summer's sun and rains have ripened the fruit, the blackberries will be alluring again, and the numbers of blossoms this year suggests that they will be abundant. Shiny and succulent, blackberries dangle just out of reach somehow. The plumpest and shiniest of them is always deepest in the thicket, and gatherers of blackberries must be bold, indeed, if they are after more than a handful to munch on. Those are particularly delicious – four or five blackberries still warm from the sun, and lightly staining fingers and lips.

But a juicy blackberry cobbler is that much better, and it is not an impossible task to gather enough berries for a cobbler as long as one is suitably clad in long pants and a long-sleeved shirt, and willing to be scratched a little.

Menemsha and Aquinnah offer fine blackberrying, and there is a little in Vineyard Haven in the Lagoon woods. It is satisfying to gather any berry in the wild, but the quest for blackberries is so challenging that when they are finally in the basket or bucket, or – better yet – on the dining room table, the gatherer feels the joy of triumph as well as the delight in consuming them.

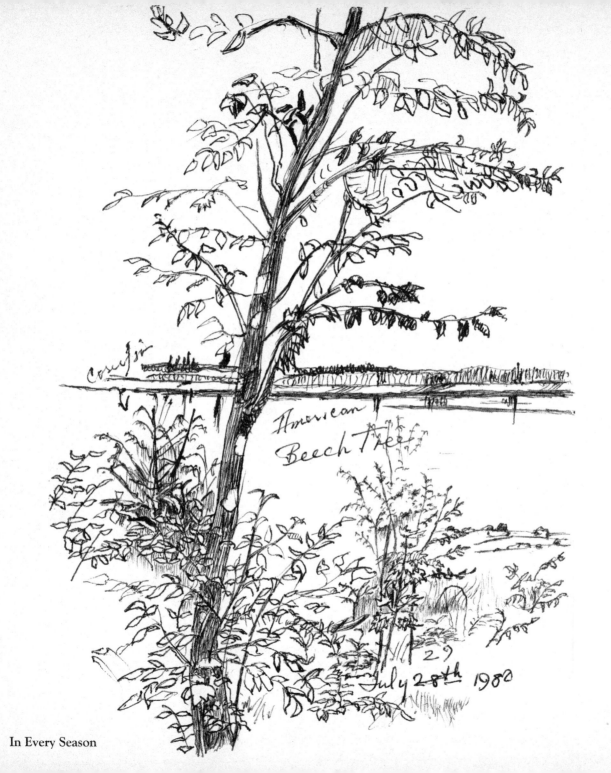

Conifir

American
Beech Tree

29
July 28th 1980

Traveling the Treetops

These between-season days before the snow falls are a perfect time for exploring fields and woods and looking closely at roadsides. In spring and summer, one cannot see the trees for the leaves. Stone walls, similarly, are hidden behind the greenery.

In September and October, though tree trunks and boughs begin to emerge as the leaves fall, it is the leaves themselves – gold, crimson, chartreuse, bronze, red – that catch our eye rather than the shapes beneath them. Then comes winter, and trunks and limbs and walls take on fantastic shapes as they are embellished by the snow.

But just now, tree trunks are gray or softly pink under early morning and evening skies. Some stand tall. Some are gracefully bowed. One that I have seen is so perfectly twisted that it could be a carved Baroque column. Tree limbs extend out and up at all angles.

In high-up tree notches, I am noticing squirrel nests. They're not neatly built at all, but higgledy-piggledy with stray twigs and leaves sticking out. They are big and seem so precariously set that I wonder that even squirrels can jump in and out of them.

For the first time, I am noticing oaks with the bark flayed off and I wonder what weather or animal has affected them. If the bark were damaged down low, I would suspect hungry deer, but more often the area stripped of its bark is more than halfway up the tree.

Now it is clear that some trees lean comfortably and cozily on others. Of course, not all of them – even deciduous trees – are bare at this time of year. Beeches still are tawny. As for the evergreens, they stand out as they never do in leafy seasons, and I am grateful for the color that they bring.

Here and there along West Tisbury roadsides, I am discovering hollies that are new to me – their dark green polished leaves gleaming against stone walls.

As for the walls themselves, I admire them at all times of year, but it is only now that I can see the lichen maps of continents and oceans on them.

I find this moment between fall and winter a peaceful time of year. It demands little of me. It does not require that I admire it the way spring does, tantalizing the eye with new buds, the nose with floral scents. It does not demand that I enjoy it, as summer does with the unspoken invitation of warmth out of doors, or as autumn does with its bright colors. This is a moment for viewing what one misses in the dramatic seasons.

Of Cats and Boats
and Bittersweet

Tuesday was a potpourri morning. There is no other way to describe it. It was a morning when I walked along the Lagoon, and sights and thoughts tumbled so swiftly I could barely keep up with them. Perhaps it was because I have been away, not watching the change of seasons day by day, so there was so much to catch up with.

When I left a month ago for England and Wales, the grapes were just ripening on our Vineyard Haven fence. Here and there, beach plums could be found at Aquinnah. The goldenrod was at its peak.

But now, autumn is in its glory. The pumpkins are ripe in our garden. I can see that the ground cherries are yellow in their jack-o'-lantern cases. The marigolds are fat. Though the goldenrod is gone, clusters of lavender wild asters have taken its place on hills and banks and shore, and the bittersweet is a tangle of gold and yellow. The beech leaves look like golden saucers.

The Canada geese were honking at sundown nearby when I went away. Now they are feasting elsewhere, but I surprised two mallards swimming purposefully this morning, making their neat V-shaped wakes on the still Lagoon.

I like sunrise, but I rarely have the energy to greet it. In these immediate post-travel days, though, as I adjust from one time zone to another, I find I am stirring before sunrise, and so I can be up and about as the apricot or lemon of morning seeps over the horizon. The oak trees of Oak Buffs are limned black against the lightening sky, and, gradually, the black velvet water becomes lighter, turning to silver, then platinum.

I thought this morning that I would turn over the rowboat I had left right side up when I went away, dump out the water, and enjoy the sunup rowing down to the shellfish hatchery. But when I climbed down the bank and reached the beach, I found that the boat was gone. It had, it seemed, chafed at its line with the rise and fall of the tide. Much of the frayed line remained, but no boat.

Last winter, the boat disappeared, too. That time, I suspect, it was taken by young mariners, for there was a single broken oar in it when I discovered it lodged beneath a pier half a mile away. My first thought this time was to head there again, but the tide was high, and there was more shore for walking if I turned toward the head of the Lagoon. And, happily, as I walked in that direction, I found the skiff hauled up into the woods only a house away from ours where neither tide nor human could easily dislodge it. And I am grateful to whatever neighbor did the hauling for me. So I

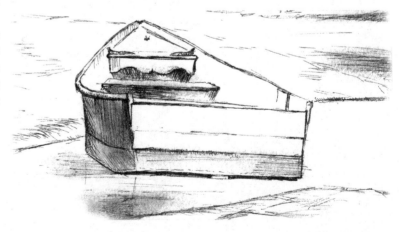

laid down my oars, for the boat was perfectly imprisoned for the winter now, and would stay right where it was until next spring brought on the urge to "go to sea" again.

Headed as I was, however, toward Barnes Road on the Oak Bluffs side of the water, I continued on my way. And, thinking kind thoughts about the boat-rescuing neighbor, I thought gratefully, too, of the neighbor who had found Groucho, our calico cat, after she had disappeared one night in a thunderstorm and been gone for days. Our neighbor, Neb Culin, looking out his bathroom window as he shaved, saw something black and orange and white in the underbrush. He had heard that Groucho was missing and called. Happily, she was quickly retrieved and, since then, has been something of a stay-at-home cat, enjoying snoozing in the sun on the windowsill. So, as I am grateful to our nautical neighbor so I am to our cat-finding neighbor.

Into this morning potpourri of thoughts, the late Donal MacPhee of Edgartown – learned friend, newspapering colleague – came, too, for we often talked of this and that, of Vineyard seasons and foreign shores, when I returned from travel somewhere and stopped by for a visit. And I thought of indomitable Mary Alley of West Tisbury, whom I will not be seeing anymore and of Captain Donald Poole of Menemsha who is gone now, too. Fall always seems a reckoning time. The leaves, in the nature of their final burst of beauty before death, cannot help but put one in mind of human friends who have just gone.

By then, I had reached the pumping station and a sprightly teenaged cygnet – gray among three snowy white adult swans – brightened my frame of mind. Last year, raccoons or skunks attacked the swans' nest and destroyed the eggs. This season, at least one youngster has survived.

As I turned back toward the Vineyard Haven side of the Lagoon, Dave Frantz was readying to go to Falmouth in his boat, and stopped for a moment as he put his oars into his skiff. I had questions to ask about the reek – the wraith-like mist that hovered above the pond last Thursday morning. Meteorologists, he told me, call it Arctic smoke. I quite like that name. It comes, he explained, when cold air hits warm water. Of course, there was more to his explanation than that, but that sufficed for my needs.

So there is Thursday's potpourri – of cats and boats and bittersweet and of old friends, of ducks and swans, of grapes and golden beech leaves, of Martha's Vineyard in the fall.

Groucho

Those Autumn Berries

The edible wild berries of summer are long gone. For blueberries, huckleberries, blackberries in fields and woods, one must wait for another July. But the decorative wild berries of fall have arrived. Bittersweet and bayberry are brightening fields and woods and redberry is in swampy places. Weekend visitors to the Island, city-bound, often seek to capture a bit of the country by carrying home autumn berry bouquets. It is a pretty business – a car's rear window filled with the red and gold of bittersweet tendrils, the silver of bayberry, or a foot passenger on the ferry with a clutch of wild berries in hand. Though the gold casing of the bittersweet is fragile, and easily broken off, if it can be preserved; bittersweet makes the cheeriest of autumn mementoes of the Vineyard in the bleakness of winter. And what could be more pleasant on a cold evening than the fragrance of bayberry – the genuine, not the artificial candle variety – perfuming apartment air.

Names on the Land

Newcomers to the Island are wont to scratch their heads with curiosity as they learn that the ferry is entering Vineyard Haven harbor between East and West Chop.

For most people, "chop" is used in conjunction with pork or lamb to suggest a cut of meat. To a few, a "chop" is the carved stone the Chinese use to stamp their names on official documents. To sailors, a "chop" in the water is caused by variable wind bringing white caps. The arms of land surrounding Vineyard Haven harbor are named East "Chop" and West "Chop" since they resemble the chops that one licks.

But Eugene Green and William Sachse in their book, *Names on the Land,* came up with the information that in fifteenth-century England, "chops" were simply divisions of land.

It is they who also pointed out that in Revolutionary days, when British Major General Sir Charles Grey was raiding the Island, he had his men take away sheep, cattle, money – everything they could manage. Happily, East and West Chop were left behind because he couldn't carry them. How fortunate we were!

Autumn Color

Autumn is here now and I have mixed feelings about it. For all its beauty, it has never been my favorite season. I do not dislike it because it presages winter. Winter – especially when the Island takes on new and mysterious contours in snow – is my favorite of all the seasons.

Cocroft - 47

Nor do I dislike fall because it signals the end of summer, since summer, nowadays – with all of its crowds – is my least favorite time of the year. But it does signal the end rather than the beginning, and, therefore, there is a melancholy quality to the fall. I am enjoying its color, however – the maple trees on Music Street whose west-facing leaves turn red long before those facing east, the goldenrod gleaming in fields, orange pumpkins, purple asters, fat brown cattails along the Lagoon, the carpet of yellow beech leaves in the Cedar Tree Neck woods. As the leaves fall, I like seeing the shapes of stalwart tree trunks and of graceful limbs revealed again. At dusk the other evening, a company of trees in Union gray were marching along beside a road.

I like the smells of fall. Although there is no longer the pungent odor of leaves burning because such burning has been banned, there is still the fragrance of wood smoke from fireplaces once there is a chill in the air. The wild grapes have gone by, but a few weeks ago, in the right woodsy places, their winey fragrance was in the air.

I find the autumn sky a crisper blue than the sky of summer and the clouds seem whiter than in summertime when there may be a haze in the air.

Canada geese are sweeping through the sky and feeding in gold-bronze fields. Wild turkey families seem to be strutting in greater numbers than usual. One must be on the alert at dusk for deer crossing roads.

When I set out early in the morning, copses are filled with birds whose songs I wish I could recognize. (In an effort to do so a few years ago, I bought a "singing" clock that had been made in China. It turned out that the hourly songs that accompanied the bird pictures were the songs of Chinese birds and were of no help at all.)

And last week I went on an autumn sail in my little boat, Blue Beard. It almost convinced me to like the fall. Tim Foote of Chilmark and I set out in mid-afternoon. The sun was shining and there seemed a reasonable amount of wind for a sail on Deep Bottom Cove in Tisbury Great Pond. We breezed along happily past Tississa where the cormorants like to sit and sun. Tim pointed out how much they resemble Daumier drawings of lawyers. Three swans bobbed into view.

Our destination was to be Town Cove into which we had once sailed by mistake and made all sorts of discoveries of old pond-front houses that cannot be easily seen from the land. But by the time we had passed the sunning cormorants, our wind was dying down. It seemed wiser to head for South Beach that lay just ahead rather than go exploring.

We beached the boat just below the Old Cut and weighted down a bow line with a timber Tim found on the beach. Then we crossed over to the seaside to sun for awhile and – as it tuned out – to watch the orange and black monarch butterflies flitting among the dune grasses. I suppose they are just about ready for their flight of thousands of miles to Mexico. Considering the journey that lies ahead, the butterflies that we saw fluttering about in the wind above the dunes seemed quite carefree. There seemed to be almost too much wind for such delicate creatures,

but Tim noticed that the wind that Blue Beard needed to get us home was dying down, now almost gone, so we returned to the boat and headed back.

Indeed, the wind was very light; it was becoming hazy in a summery sort of way and the landscape we slowly passed did not resemble the landscape we had passed sailing out. The judicial cormorants, for example, were on the wrong side of the cove. Houses that we thought ought to be on the headlands were not and boats and houses we did not remember seemed to be there instead. Meanwhile, the wind was barely a breeze and the water a glassy calm. Happily, we had one broken oar aboard and Tim began paddling. Unsure as we were in the haze of where we were going, we contemplated what we would do if we were again in the wrong cove.

Happily, we had not made a mistake, but the sun was setting – blazing red as it went down, when we finally reached our destination. By the time that Blue Beard had been made fast and the sails furled, the moon was glowing gold in the east, but the pond was crimson from the sun going down in the west It was another of those times when autumn was showing off – making a point of proving how beautiful a season it can be. There was nothing melancholy about it at all.

Golden Path to Fall

This is the time for wild ducks and Canada geese, and deer browsing, and so, on Monday, I set off for the Felix Neck Wildlife Sanctuary after those sure autumn signs. Up-Island, I could have found them almost anywhere, but Down-Island, where I am living now, Felix Neck seemed most likely to have them all . . .

The sanctuary's wild turkeys were intent on foraging under a bayberry bush. The foraging must have been good, indeed, for every now and then I could hear a contented gup-gup-gupping sound. One of the toms watched over his flock, keeping an eye out for intruders rather than foraging much himself. He gave me a glance or two, but quickly turned back to his charges. In the bright morning sun, his feathers glistened.

I have never paid much attention to wild turkeys before – although the flock near Craig Kingsbury's used to amuse me in the days when they crossed the State Road and perched on the stone wall above Lake Tashmoo. So I stood for awhile watching the Felix Neck turkeys claw the earth with their feet, dislodging succulent morsels from under branches and leaves. And I thought, as I watched, how primitive a turkey looks with its small bluish-white head with red carbuncles on it, the snood on the back of the tom's beak when it is courting, and the stringy beard dangling from his neck.

After a time, the flock apparently exhausted the supply of seeds and insects beneath the bayberry bush and was hungry for acorns, or else the impatient tom simply decided that they should all move on, or he turned and strode off across the field toward the sanctuary then, and the flock obediently followed. He stretched his wings and they stretched theirs.

Watching them, I contemplated the field where a few desultory lavender wild asters were still blooming and goldenrod was turning brown. And suddenly, I realized how much of the late summer and of fall's beginnings I have missed this year, for I have been traveling. It is too late, of course to make amends for what has passed me by, but not too late to look ahead to changes in the fields and flowers. My eye was caught then by the crimson patches of sumac and huckleberry, and then I found some fat milkweed pods that had not yet burst and spun out their silky thread. I assisted. I tore one apart and touched the threads of silk inside and sent them catapulting out to deposit their nut-brown seed. But there was almost no wind in the still morning so the seed simply wafted down to an everlasting plant.

Oct. 16th, 1976

I followed a trail to the duck pond next, plucking a stalk of timothy as I walked and putting it between my teeth. Pine needles, I decided as I thoughtfully chewed, are by far the best year-round confection of this sort, for they are sweet and juicy at any time of year. Timothy lacks juiciness in the fall.

The duck pond bustled with mallards and widgeons, and I thought I saw one canvasback, but I am not sure. One swan chased another and a teenaged cygnet with a neck that still bore the gray plumage of youth plunged its head and neck into the water and thrashed it from side to side in some strange, almost ceremonial way. There was much quacking and beating of the water with wings, and throaty clucking. A late arrival duck hurried from the far end of the pond to be near where the others were gathered for their breakfast, and his wake rippled the silver-gold water. Then, overhead, was the insistent honking of Canada geese and five of them plummeted commandingly into the pond. Beyond it a bit was a pretty pine grove with the sunlight making Oriental rug-like geometric patterns.

To my delight, in a patch of sand was the clear imprint of a deer's hoof. Where the woods were damp, six toadstools grew, their tops mahogany-colored, and I could not help thinking they looked like polished dining tables where elves might just have finished breakfasting. Indeed, some of the tables had been overturned in the elves' haste to be about their business.

In another pine grove, Indian pipes were growing. As I recall, Indian pipes thrive among dead things, and surely they have a bloodless look about them, so I passed them quickly and went out into an open, sunny field again. There, the leaves of wild cherry added a blush to the meadow.

A touch of more vivid pink in the marshlands that abut Sengekontacket Pond attracted me and I made my way toward it. I found that it was twig-like glasswort I had noticed. By then, mid-morning was approaching, and so, with a twig in this pocket, a sprig of everlasting in my hand, I made my way back to the barn. And my heart was light.

Coroft
Apr. 1977

Snow at Last!

At last, the Vineyard has seen a snowfall this winter! Apparently, I missed the best of it that fell on Sunday night, for I was off Island then. But Monday morning, I am told, early risers awoke to find that gray-limbed trees and tan-brown fields were dazzling white. Fences and stonewalls and rural mailboxes, of course, were similarly transformed. In New York City, where I had spent the weekend, there was gray mush in the streets when I went out, and I longed for the squeak my boots made in a fresh Island snow and their crunching sound after a crust had formed. Indeed, when I heard that there had been a Vineyard snowfall, I was so filled with longing for it that I cut short plans to go farther south to Washington and came back to the Island instead.

It was all foolishness, I know, but since there has been no snow at all this winter, and March has now arrived, it seemed unlikely that I would have a chance to see snow on the Island any other time. I took the first bus after I had made my decision and hoped the snow would not melt, but await my arrival. Not only did it, but the following morning, I was greeted with a fresh snowfall.

Admittedly, it was not a grand one, and Sunday night's had not been either – only two to three inches, at best – but enough to create a new landscape, the way a snowfall always does.

I went out, of course, in Tuesday's snow as soon as I was up. There was ice by my back steps and I tried, first, to sprinkle fireplace ashes on it to make it less slippery. Then I remembered that, up Tiasquam Road where I live, Tom Hodgson, guardian of the road, keeps a pile of sand to help out travelers in snow emergencies. So, with a Cronig's bag and a fireplace shovel in hand, I set out on the road after a little sand. Halfway up, however, I changed my route, for, there, in front of me, was the inviting path through the woods to Glimmerglass Pond.

I had not been down it all winter, but someone else had been, for there were footsteps and dog prints in the snow. I was sorry not to be the first to make snow tracks, but, at least, there were only the three of us – the man and dog, and later me. I suspected it was Dan Cabot and his Lab, Cassie, for they live near Glimmerglass.

The pond was ominously black with the white snow around it and gray sky overhead. Often, there are ducks on it, or a Canada goose or two, and there used to be swans. But there were none of these Tuesday morning. There were, however, rabbit tracks and, once I had quit the pond and started across the field toward the Middle Road, I followed a path of deer tracks. Once, several winters ago, after a real snowstorm, I lost my way on this very same route and found myself crawling beneath snow-laden limbs into mysterious territory. How curious it was to have lost my way that time in virtually my own backyard!

This time, the snow cover was too light for me to lose my way, but pleasant soft flakes fell on my nose and on the flowered white scarf – a babushka that was given to me long ago in Russia – that covered my head. I know it is not stylish to wear a scarf

over my head (though Jackie Kennedy Onassis always seemed to in casual photographs), but I find a scarf the best possible sort of head covering. It can be pulled forward to shield one's eyes from either snow or sun, and even in a rainfall, a woolen babushka provides reasonably good head coverage.

With my Cronig's bag and my fireplace shovel still underneath my arm, I followed the deer cracks across the field. Crows were cawing. In the woods across the Middle Road, a woodpecker pecked and I heard a cardinal's call. It was a happy sound and I wondered if the cardinal was as pleased as I to have a snowfall. I doubted it since snow, of course, covers the seeds a bird likes on the ground. On the other hand, a snowfall shows off the bright red plumage of a cardinal so well. It must be pleasing to be so well displayed.

My walk was not a long one, and I did end up, finally, at the bin full of sand. Indeed, it had sufficient snow cover in it so that I thought, at first, Tom was no longer keeping a sand pile for emergencies, but when I dug through the snow, there was sand, indeed. I filled my sack and headed home.

By then, my two orange cats were out exploring. They lack my enthusiasm for the snow, though I have had some cats who reveled in it almost as much as I do, and a collie dog that was even more daft than I about frolicking in the snow and would dig his long golden nose into it, only to withdraw it for a mighty sneeze.

I sprinkled the sand in front of the back steps. The snow had almost stopped then. It hadn't, indeed, been a Vineyard snowfall of consequence. But I did not regret for a minute that I had hurried some 200 miles back from New York City for a taste of it.

A Walk in the Snow

Yesterday was a wondrous winter day – a day that began with a touch of snow that soon was a full-fledged snowstorm, with the snow that had fallen soft and deep. It was surely a day for walking. Snow days always are. It was a day of discovery. Snow days are that, too – days when familiar forms no longer are so familiar – when, watchful though we may be, it is easy to lose our way among the strange new shapes the snow has sculpted. I was not up to see the sun rise, though I had been the day before when the sky was beribboned with pink, the Lagoon below our house glowing, reflecting the pink. That day, I had heard the first cawing of the

crows, the twitter of waking birds. The mourning doves on the limbs outside our kitchen window shifted their wings and raised their heads a bit to see what the morning had in store.

I followed a rabbit's track through the woods and down to the shore. There, I could follow the tracks no farther, for the rabbit had hopped into a cozy place beneath a porch.

So I made my way without the companionship of tracks along the shore where the seaweed in the first light was sparkling with giant ice flowers, the Lagoon ice itself in volcanic upheaval. Blond grasses arched against the ice.

Faster than I would have liked, the sun was up – the Lagoon no longer a blaze of red, but instead all silver and gold. Here and there on the bluffs above, white smoke swirled from chimneys. Lights began to go on in houses. It was time for everyone to be abroad. A door opened and closed. A dog barked. A chorus of ducks quacked as I neared their swimming hole in the ice.

I surprised sparrows in a copse and they flew away toward the aqua sky. Then suddenly three shapes – I thought they were dogs – came into view along the ice floe. Worried that they might fall into the cold pond, I whistled anxiously and crunched through the snow and the bare bayberry bushes to get closer. An angry seagull was watching them, too, annoyed at their invasion of its fishing territory. And well he might have been, for a closer inspection revealed three otters fishing, then climbing back onto the ice, then diving again, shaking their prey, nuzzling each other, arching their backs. I watched the otters for half an hour or so, then turned back toward home, elated at my discovery.

But today I rose later – too late, it seemed, for the otters. Instead, I watched a pair of mallards fly to the open water where the otters had been. As the snow fell, it transformed tree stumps into Easter Island statues, tree limbs into hiding places for slithering white snakes, miniature crouching snow leopards, albino crocodiles, and the like – all stretched out.

In the middle of the day, when the snowfall was heaviest, I stayed indoors, but by 4 p.m., I was lured out again. In the morning, there had been wind. By afternoon, it had died down and the woodland landscape, with no wind shaking the trees, looked as if it was all Belgian lace, crocheted with care. And the shrubs suddenly were abloom with snowy hydrangeas.

Last week, I was woods walking with a native of Maine. She was talking rather disparagingly, I thought, about the snow quality in southern New England versus that in the north. The next time there is a snowfall, I must invite her to go walking along the Lagoon with me, and otter viewing, while our snow is still fresh.

A Beach Walker's Treasury

February is a good time for walking on beaches. They begin to be just warm enough to set out without thick mittens and fur-lined boots. Although there are always some fellow beach walkers, it is still possible to find a shore where you can be almost alone. For me, that is an essential element of satisfying beach exploring.

If you are out to beach-comb, you don't want company, for generosity should not extend to sharing iridescent shell treasures or driftwood fish with knothole eyes. Like placer gold, beach discoveries are for the finder to cherish.

Recently, I walked along the Katama shore in Edgartown. Although it was midday, there were not too many abroad. There were four dogs tussling, one person to speak to, and three others far away. I watched the waves roll in and curl, shadowing the water beneath the curls to an emerald green.

I had never noticed the variety of shades of green in the sea before that Sunday. It was yellow-green where the sun lit it, gray-green where it did not, blue-green where it reflected the sky, and emerald in the wave troughs. And the spindrift was glistening – blue and pink and lavender clusters of bubbles along the shore after the seas had broken and gone out again. There was not much combing to do. The sand was bare of anything but a handful of shells, a driftwood root, and one tree limb, but it was a good day for beach-walking and remembering childhood walks along South Beach when my father pointed out to sea and told me that Spain was over there, and I squinted hard in hopes of finding it, and made cups of my hands around my eyes so I could see the way binoculars do.

Now that I am a traveler, I have stood on Spanish shores since, and peered out across the Atlantic and wondered if Martha's Vineyard was out there somewhere. I have trailed my fingers in the water and tried to calculate, if his geography was correct, how long it had taken that water to make its way from South Beach to the shore at Santander.

Four weeks later at Lambert's Cove in West Tisbury, the combing was better, though it was a lowering day, and the rain spat now and then and sent me huddling under dunes and on a cottage porch. To my delight, the rain soon dissuaded the other beach walkers. I found a place where the inlet to James Pond was too deep for crossing. I looked for a spot with a stony bottom and waded over and started up toward Paul's Point. Beyond the inlet, there were no footprints in the sand, which meant I was in virgin territory. The only tracks were bird tracks hurrying down

to the water's edge. Bird tracks always seem to me to be hurrying somehow. I ambled for a while along the wrack line; then I found a sheltered niche for myself in an oatmeal-textured boulder, and sat down to survey the beach I was planning to explore.

Mike Zoll, a Vineyard Haven poet, told me he walks on beaches because of the sense of eternity they give. "When I walk on a beach," he says, in more or less these words, "I know that when I turned over in bed this morning the sea was there; while I got dressed, it was there. Last night it was there, and the sea wind was blowing, and the clouds were scudding. Walking a beach, I know how small a part I am of how great a universe."

Another friend says he walks beaches because of the adventure of it, the unexpected around each dune and cape and bluff. I think that is why I beach-walk. I looked down the beach and saw a few hunks of wood washed up and a telegraph pole whose tarred surface was red-black in the rain. There was also a "No Trespassing" sign with John T. Daggett's name on it. Wave action at the base of the cliffs must have caused the bluff to collapse and made the sign and the pole tumble down from the top.

Farther on, I walked in the wrack, sometimes near the water where I could hear the stones growling and grating as the waves hurled them in. Higher up on the shore, though, was where the flotsam and jetsam had been tossed – tufts of aqua lobster-pot line, two smashed pots, a red and white buoy, a door with heavy hinges, a plywood board caught between boulders. The sand was striated by the wind into zigzag and Marcel-wave patterns.

I passed a cottage on the bluff, just as the rain began to tap on my Sou'wester hat again, so I climbed up toward the porch. Checked curtains at the windowpanes, though faded, looked hospitable. I waited there until the blackest of the storm clouds had passed and then ambled on. Beside the cottage was a Y-shaped tree washed up. The shape would have been just right as David's slingshot when he fought Goliath.

There were boat shells and mussel shells and an occasional razor clam shell. I passed the tail end of a horseshoe crab and a skate egg case. Skate egg cases have always seemed much too disagreeable to me – dry and dusty-black – to merit so delightful a name as mermaid's purse. I picked up a string of knobbed whelk egg-cases. Later, Mrs. C. D. J. Smith of Oak Bluffs asked me if I had ever opened one, and when I said I hadn't, she slit one of the papery disks open for me and a dozen miniature whelks, not even as large as the white of a fingernail, but perfectly formed, fell out.

On the beach, there were a few old shoes, too – a tennis shoe, a rubber sandal, a man's leather shoe. I picked them up and looked inside to see if they might have exotic markings that would suggest that they had fallen overboard from a foreign trawler. But the markings were all washed away.

I found a handful of shotgun shells, red ones and green ones. But there were two good finds. One was a murderously sharp hook that I took to be a boat hook and later learned it was for gaffing fish – getting bluefish, sharks, or any other fish that comes alongside a boat on board. The other find was the side of a boat with timbers so enormous that I could not help wondering how the waves could have been strong enough to drive it in. The fastenings were as fat as eels; the timbers as thick as my wrist to my elbow. I shuddered as I walked along beside it, examining it. Whose boat had she been? From where had she sailed? Who might have been aboard when she was wrecked? My brother wonders, from my description of her size, if she might have been a rum-runner long buried in the offshore sand, churned up by last month's storm.

And that was enough beach-combing for this day. I watched the wind tug at a seagull's tail where the gull perched on a shore-side rock. But he was discomfited and flew away. I turned to head back, too.

Animal Tracking

This wintry winter, I have been snow-walking mornings. I go out soon enough after the snowfall so that my footprints and those of a few animals and birds, are the only tracks. I am likely to be first greeted, of course, in these days of wild turkey flocks up-Island and down, by a dozen of them perched on my West Tisbury fence or pecking hungrily through the snow in the garden. I know I should feel sorry for them these cold days and fling out grain, but it would attract the smaller birds my cats attack. And I cannot quite forgive, either, the turkeys' summertime ravaging of my strawberry and blueberry patches. So I pass them by with rarely a nod as I set out on my favorite walk. It takes me, first, from my side yard off Music Street across the Tiasquam River. There, if I am early enough, I rouse a mallard feeding.

Accompanied by the cawing of the crows, I head up a slight hill into the woods, climb down a rocky bank, and cross the Glimmerglass Pond waterfall. Next, I pass through a canopy of high brush beside the pond. In summer, there are often swans on the water and water lilies bobbing. Of course, the lilies are long gone, but the swans may simply be far away across the ice. Most mornings, in a house on the pond bank, there is an inviting, cozy light in a window. Though I enjoy my solitary walk, it is nice to know that someone else is up, and I can almost smell the fragrance from the coffee pot. A wire-haired fox terrier used to live in that house and often he would bound out energetically through a wire gate and, wagging his tail, join me on the rest of my meandering.

This takes me across what is, in spring, a swampy place best crossed on a plank bridgeway. At this time of year, of course, one simply crunches through the snow across it. Next comes a wide expanse of field with golden grass tufts poking through the snow, and, if it is fresh snow, there are always bird and animal tracks to follow.

Ascertaining what the creatures are that inhabit wood and field has always fascinated me. Since going on a walking safari in Zimbabwe recently, where I was following the tracks of elephants and warthogs, Cape buffalo and zebras, track-following has become an especially interesting pastime – inadequate identifier though I am.

I carry with me A Field Guide to Animal Tracks, and if I'm not mistaken, a muskrat frequents the field and water's edge, for there is a telltale slithery line in the snow between one set of tracks. The picture in the book calls what these resemble "muskrat tracks in light snow, on ice, running gait." I think that's what they are, but, alternatively, they may simply be the tracks of a meadow vole, for the picture under "vole" bears a close resemblance to the tracks I see.

But of rabbit tracks I am certain. One can feel the hippity-hop of them set deep in the snow. As for the bird tracks, deducing what bird made them is impossible for me.

In Zimbabwean game parks, guides were often decrying poaching – in particular of the black rhinoceros whose horn is highly valued in the Orient for aphrodisiacs and in Yemen for sheiks' daggers. Its value nowadays is far higher than that of gold. As a result, poachers follow the rhino tracks assiduously, seeking their illegal game. My brief experience in Vineyard tracking suggests that, as a poacher, I would surely be a washout.

When I cross the field on my morning jaunts, I arrive at the Middle Road. Sometimes I turn left toward the Panhandle and go on farther, taking a back road through the Whiting field, and, occasionally, I see the tracks of deer in the snow there. I am more secure about recognizing hoof marks than footprints of voles and moles and mice. But even if I am wrong in my identifications, my morning tracking makes for a pleasant half hour or so out of doors on a wintry Vineyard morning.

Though I travel extensively around the world, that intimate beauty of a frosted Island wood, a dark green pine limb sweeping the snow, a frozen pond, white fields untouched except for tracks of wildlife, I find matchless.

T.C.

Sea and Snow

Last week, after our snowfall, I went walking. I always try to beat the plows and the sanders and, for awhile, I did. The only sounds were the squeaking snow beneath my boots and the wind soughing. It was just about dusk and a bird or two was uttering a goodnight chirp before tucking its head under its wing. The snow along West Tisbury's Music Street, gleaming under occasional street lights, seemed to me like that "ribbon of moonlight" in Alfred Noyes' poem, "The Highwayman." But then, as I ambled dreamily, I heard the rumble of the plow and it barreled down the road driving me off it into deeper snow and the sander followed fouling the ribbon of road with its brown sand.

And so, the next day, seeking to escape them, I set off across a Whiting field. The snow was still pristinely white and untouched – except by rabbits who had left their tracks and deer whose hoof prints I found now and then.

As is often the case after a snowfall, I lost my way, even though I was in familiar territory. Every now and then, I crunched through a patch of ice into a hidden puddle or I caught myself sliding on the ice under the snow. But the sight before me – of an endless white field brightened by brown-gold grass – was just what I had been looking for.

Which do I prefer, the blue sea of summer or white snow of winter extending as far as the eye can see? Both sea and snow, when they are quiet after a storm soothe. Of course a tumultuous wind may have brought the sea high up onto the sand and combers may have thundered and crashed bringing the water in. Similarly, in a blizzard, a strong wind brings the snow and drives it into drifts. But the ferocity of the wind is easily forgotten once it has abated and the sea is quietly lapping or the snow is softly spread.

When I quit the snowy field, I was on the Panhandle road. Again, it was dusk. I looked up at the trees against a darkening gray sky. The snow, by then, was all gone from them and I was seeing them in all their bareness. In summer, the shapes of branches cannot be seen under their green leaves.

In winter, the elephant gray limbs stand out – some stretching in a gentle way across a road, seeking, it seems, to touch the tree limbs that are reaching out in the same way from the other side. Others, gnarled, look angry at being without the greenery that hides their imperfections.

Which do I prefer – summer days when the sea tends to be soothing, days when the sun is warm, the trees leafy and the fields bedecked with wild flowers, or winter days after a snow?

The choice is not easy. But I suspect I lean toward the latter. Perhaps I am just contrary, but an untouched field of snow, trees limned against it, animal tracks to keep me company, snow-covered roads winding mysteriously, the crisp air of winter, and the inviting smell of smoke from wood fires bring me the greatest solace. I have been enjoying this snowy Vineyard winter.

T. Cocroft - 1971

Choosing Favorites

I am recently back from travels in Scandinavia and friends are asking "Which country did you like the best?" It is a question I have never been able to answer, but on Sunday when the sky over the Vineyard was such a radiant blue, the goldenrod was glowing in fields, Chilmark's North Road was dappled with sunlight and the beach plums were a powdery purple along Moshup's Trail at Aquinnah, I altered my friends' question and asked myself, "What on the Vineyard do you like the best?" Is it the moors of Chilmark looming in the mist, trees arched into arcades over up-Island roads, the gingerbread on Oak Bluffs' Camp Ground cottages, spinnakers billowing on Katama Bay, mossy boulders at Indian Hill, stone walls a-tumble in West Tisbury?

I could, of course, no more answer the question I had posed to myself than my friends' question.

Sunday morning, when I was at Chilmark's Beetlebung Corner, I was certain there was no lovelier Island place then Chilmark. Along the North Road, there are still relatively few houses. Those that there are, have a stable, well-settled air. They tend to be old farmhouses that are a trifle rundown. If there are flowers in their dooryards, they are not in tailored gardens. When there are fences, they are old-fashioned picket fences painted white.

On Friday, on the South Road, as I crossed the bridge at Quitsa, and I looked out onto the pond where small boats bobbed, my choice was confirmed.

But later I went picking beach plums on the West Basin Road in Aquinnah. The sunset glowed apricot and fairly burst across the sky, I startled a striped cat with a mouse and later a rabbit that bounded away into the undergrowth, with his tail signaling his route.

They put me in mind of East Chop, where I spent my childhood summers with a collie dog and a white cat with one black ear and a black tail. That cat, too, was a mouser, while the dog took the greatest delight in chasing rabbits under the wild roses along the bluffs.

Walking along the bluffs with them in the evening, I would watch the moonlight shimmering silver on the Sound, the Cape's lights sparkling like stars, the stars themselves. If it was foggy, there was a ghostliness in the air and the warning beam from the East Chop light would be softly diffused. And though I walk by the lighthouse less frequently now than when I was young, I still find great beauty on the East Chop bluffs.

Then there is Ocean Park in Oak Bluffs that has always been a favorite of mine with its plantings, its overlook to the Sound, the bandstand sitting so proudly, the circle of houses with wide porches and giant rocking chairs, and the touches of gingerbread.

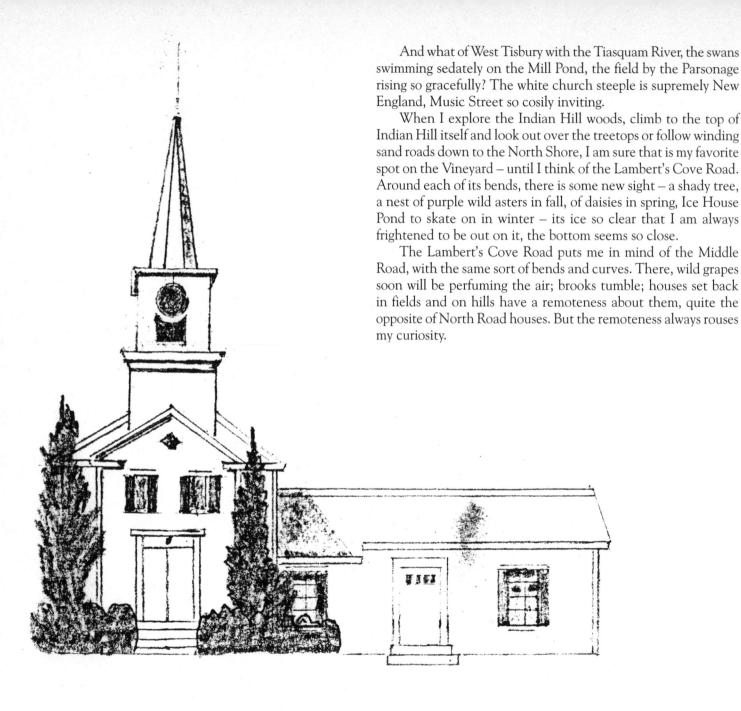

And what of West Tisbury with the Tiasquam River, the swans swimming sedately on the Mill Pond, the field by the Parsonage rising so gracefully? The white church steeple is supremely New England, Music Street so cosily inviting.

When I explore the Indian Hill woods, climb to the top of Indian Hill itself and look out over the treetops or follow winding sand roads down to the North Shore, I am sure that is my favorite spot on the Vineyard – until I think of the Lambert's Cove Road. Around each of its bends, there is some new sight – a shady tree, a nest of purple wild asters in fall, of daisies in spring, Ice House Pond to skate on in winter – its ice so clear that I am always frightened to be out on it, the bottom seems so close.

The Lambert's Cove Road puts me in mind of the Middle Road, with the same sort of bends and curves. There, wild grapes soon will be perfuming the air; brooks tumble; houses set back in fields and on hills have a remoteness about them, quite the opposite of North Road houses. But the remoteness always rouses my curiosity.

And how I would miss Menemsha if it were not there with its fat green trawlers and swordfishing boats and mounds of scallop shells, its lobster pots and fishy smells and swordfish tails.

The other morning I walked from Zack's Cliffs in Aquinnah to the Gay Head Cliffs. Sandpipers scurried purposefully where the sea washed in and out. Beach grass arched in the wind and sketched pictures in the sand. There was no surf that particular morning and I rather wished that there were – those thundering white-maned steeds that my father told me, when I was a child, were the thoroughbreds kept by Neptune, the god of the sea, in an undersea courtyard beside his rock-walled castle. At the right time of night, my father said, you could see mermaids holding the horses' streaming manes and riding, riding.

But even without the surf, the Aquinnah breach lured me on with the sandpipers and the terns and seagulls racing the incoming tide on the sand. And I thought as the Gay Head Cliffs loomed in the distance, that I would not do without them for anything, faded though time, and the sea, and rains have made their once brilliant red and white and black clay surface. They remain as spectacular as any headland I have seen in the world.

Nov. 4, 1957

Then there are the Island's metropolises, for they nearly have become such nowadays – Vineyard Haven and Edgartown. Could I say that I prefer one to the other? Hardly, for the white clapboard houses of Spring Street and Center Street in Vineyard Haven equal some of the best of Edgartown's spacious whaling captains' dwellings. And there is a genuineness, a lived-in, purposeful quality in Vineyard Haven that I like.

I went sailing the other afternoon on Lake Tashmoo. The Canada geese were feeding; sailboats were tacking, We went down near the old Water Works where the pond was still and green. As I looked up at the treed slopes on the up-Island side, I thought for a moment that surely Lake Tashmoo was the most beautiful site on the Vineyard.

But then I remember the Lagoon and its lapping waters, the flowering trees along its shores that dip their branches into the water, the cormorants stretching their wings to dry them. What would I do with the Lagoon if I chose Lake Tashmoo as my favorite Island site?

No, there can be no answer to "What Vineyard place do I like the best?"

Beachcombers along the South Shore in winter find buoys and lines and sculpted driftwood washed in, and, on windy days, the hardy shore-walker can listen to the rumble of the stones that waves churn up at Chilmark's Squibnocket.

Time was when Vineyard winters meant ice skating on West Tisbury's Parsonage Pond and the alert might see an otter popping up through an air hole on the Mill Pond. Edgartown and Oak Bluffs eelers would be out on Sengekontacket with their spears. But global warming, sadly, seems to have done away with our ice.

A Vineyard spring – like springs everywhere – brings a faint pink blush to the trees. The greening of Fred Fisher's weeping willow by his Tisbury farm is a sure sign that spring has arrived. So are the white-pink bells on the blueberry and huckleberry bushes, snowdrops blooming, brown trout, brook trout, and rainbow trout being stocked in Seth's Pond and the Mill Pond in West Tisbury. Insects emerge from their winter nests and cocoons. Skunk cabbages erupt in damp places. There is the peeping of pinkletinks at sundown, the song of redwing blackbirds at sun-up.

Off-season, Martha's Vineyard is Nature's rather than man's realm.

About the Author and Artists

Phyllis Méras

Phyllis Méras is a longtime Martha's Vineyard resident and a former managing editor of the *Vineyard Gazette*. She was a travel editor at the *Providence Journal* and the *New York Times* and has traveled extensively around the world. She is the author of three previous books about Martha's Vineyard:

First Spring: A Martha's Vineyard Journal
Country Editor: Henry Beetle Hough and the Vineyard Gazette
Martha's Vineyard: Quiet Pleasures

She has also written travel books, cookbooks, and crafts books. She is the wife of the late Thomas H. Cocroft.

Photo by Sal Laterra

Thomas H. Cocroft

Thomas H. Cocroft was a self-taught artist whose strong landscapes and seascapes were well-known in his native Rhode Island in the 1940s, '50s and '60s. In 1969, he moved to Martha's Vineyard with his wife, Phyllis Méras; he died in 1989. He exhibited his art in Providence, Boston, the Southwest, and on the Vineyard.

Robert E. Schwartz

Robert E. Schwartz is a graduate of Columbia College and the Columbia University School of Architecture. He is a registered architect and architectural renderer as well as a landscape painter. He has exhibited at the New York Watercolor Society and on the Vineyard, and was the designer and a founder of the Field Gallery in West Tisbury. He and his wife, Maggie, were West Tisbury seasonal residents from the 1950s until 2002, when they made the Vineyard their year-round home.